M000034634

AN IDEAS INTO ACTION GUIDEBOOK

Adapting to Organizational Change

IDEAS INTO ACTION GUIDEBOOKS

Aimed at managers and executives who are concerned with their own and others' development, each guidebook in this series gives specific advice on how to complete a developmental task or solve a leadership problem.

CONTRIBUTORS	David Dinwoodie, Edward Marshall, Russ McCallian, Bertrand Sereno, Jim Shields, Sophia Zhao
DIRECTOR OF ASSESSMENTS, TOOLS, AND PUBLICATIONS	Sylvester Taylor
MANAGER, PUBLICATION DEVELOPMENT	Peter Scisco
EDITORS	Stephen Rush
	Karen Lewis
ASSOCIATE EDITOR	Shaun Martin
COPY EDITOR	Tazmen Hansen
WRITER	Martin Wilcox
DESIGN AND LAYOUT	Joanne Ferguson
COVER DESIGN	Laura J. Gibson
	Chris Wilson, 29 & Company
RIGHTS AND PERMISSIONS	Kelly Lombardino

CCL No. 457
ISBN No. 978-1-60491-160-2

CENTER FOR CREATIVE LEADERSHIP
WWW.CCL.ORG

Adapting to Organizational Change

Center for
Creative
Leadership®

THE IDEAS INTO ACTION GUIDEBOOK SERIES

This series of guidebooks draws on the practical knowledge that the Center for Creative Leadership (CCL) has generated since its inception in 1970. The purpose of the series is to provide leaders with specific advice on how to complete a developmental task or solve a leadership challenge. In doing that, the series carries out CCL's mission to advance the understanding, practice, and development of leadership for the benefit of society worldwide.

CCL's unique position as a research and education organization supports a community of accomplished scholars and educators in a community of shared knowledge. CCL's knowledge community holds certain principles in common, and its members work together to understand and generate practical responses to the ever-changing circumstances of leadership and organizational challenges.

In its interactions with a richly varied client population, in its research into the effect of leadership on organizational performance and sustainability, and in its deep insight into the workings of organizations, CCL creates new, sound ideas that leaders all over the world put into action every day. We believe you will find the Ideas Into Action Guidebooks an important addition to your leadership toolkit.

Table of Contents

In Brief

Change is a constant in today's workplace, and leaders must learn strategies to deal with change successfully, or otherwise face derailment. To succeed, you must first understand how changes within your organization are affecting you, and then use that understanding to help manage the transition from the old way to the new way of doing things. This transition typically occurs in three distinct phases: the ending, where you accept the conclusion of the old way of doing things; the neutral zone, where you begin to adapt to the confusion of the new way of doing things; and the new beginning, where you accept the new way of doing things and begin to successfully move forward in the new environment. Furthermore, by understanding how you and other individuals perceive your organization, you can gain a greater awareness of how to specifically manage the transition. Once you have done this, you will be able to move forward, helping yourself and the individuals you lead to survive and thrive.

Change and Transition

Today there seems to be very little business as usual. Turbulence is common, with organizations facing a dizzying array of changes. Many of these are small, but a significant number affect the entire organization. An organization's mission may change, as well as its focus, strategy, culture, and market. Such changes can have a serious impact on you as a leader.

Your success as a leader will very likely depend on how well you deal with such change. Research by the Center for Creative Leadership has found that successful executives adapt to the changing external pressures facing the organization, adjust management style to changing situations, accept changes as positive, revise plans as necessary, and take into account people's concerns during change. In fact, in CCL's research regarding North American and European leaders, the most frequently mentioned success factor was the ability to adapt. In describing leaders they knew, American leaders mentioned adaptability in 55 percent of the success stories that they shared, and European leaders mentioned adaptability in 67 percent of the success stories that they shared.

CCL research has also found that leaders who aren't able to adapt to change—those who show a marked resistance to change

and an inability to learn from feedback and be flexible— are likely to derail: to stop advancing or even leave the organization.

But what do you need to do in order to adapt?

First, it is imperative that you clearly understand

the difference between change and transition during times of organizational turbulence. As a leader, you will be expected not only to contend with destabilizing events within the organization but also to adjust your management style to deal with the reactions that accompany change.

Change can best be understood as the situations and occurrences that impact organizations and individuals—such as a new boss, a move to another physical location, or a shift in policy. Change typically happens quickly and most often begins with the realization that something new has begun. It creates the need to move from "the way it used to be" to "the way it is now."

Unlike change, transition is best understood as the internal psychological process of adapting to a new situation. Transition can happen quickly or slowly and is marked not by a new beginning but by the end of a previous condition. It is the process of moving successfully from the old to the new. Furthermore, change and transition often occur at the same time, which makes the ability to recognize them even more important.

Once you understand the difference between change and transition, you can take the second step: identify how the changes in the organization affect your feelings and thoughts, and focus on managing the transition. Becoming aware of these thoughts and feelings is a key aspect of adapting to change.

According to CCL feedback coaches, leaders who have experienced significant changes within their organizations react with a similar set of thoughts and feelings—although, at the time, many do not recognize the connection between them. For many of these leaders, changes within and outside their organizations challenge their experience with being right and in control. If left unresolved, the resulting self-doubts and negativity can lead otherwise successful people to derail.

Figure 1: Thoughts and Feelings about Change

Thoughts	Feelings
After all I have done for this organization, I can't believe they did this.	angry
I just know I will be fired as soon as the cost cutting starts.	fearful
Everyone but me improved his or her position in the organization.	insignificant
I used to report to the president, and now there are two layers between us.	powerless
All the power is in sales now; research and development is completely ignored.	disenfranchised
I knew that taking on this project was a waste of time; now my reputation is completely ruined.	unappreciated
I was in line for a top position, but with the new owners, I was cheated out of what I was promised.	cheated
I don't understand the language or the customs in this overseas market. I don't know what works.	frustrated
I can't possibly compete with this influx of young talent. They have too much energy for me.	intimidated
I don't think I am creative enough to get any attention in this new, faster-paced production cycle.	threatened
I can't do my old job and learn all these new procedures at the same time. It's just too much.	stressed
Learning how to do things the new company's way is making me exhausted.	tired
What am I going to do now?	helpless

However, if you are able to identify the connections between your thoughts and feelings and the impact that organizational change has on you, you will be more likely to implement and manage a smooth transition toward the current situation. To do this, you must first accept the change and then navigate the transition, while making sure that you can identify the thoughts and feelings that are impacting your ability to manage the transition smoothly. Worksheet 1, Thoughts and Feelings about Change, will help you identify your thoughts and feelings.

The third thing that is necessary in order for you to adapt to change is to note that transition typically occurs in stages. William Bridges, a leader in the field of change management, has identified three:

- **Ending.** In this stage, you mark a conclusion. You let go of a clear past, honoring and grieving the ending but accepting it and taking with you what you can.

- **Neutral zone.** In this stage, you accept the confusion of living with a clear ending but having no clear beginning. You allow clarity to develop, using creativity, renewal, and innovation to point toward a new beginning.

- **New beginning.** In this stage, you utilize the clarity that has developed in the neutral zone and accept the challenge of working in a changed environment. You are aware that a change has occurred, you realize that some things were lost and some things were gained, and you work with eyes wide open in this new environment.

This guidebook will help you learn to define each of the transition stages, recognize your thoughts and feelings associated with each stage, and develop strategies to deal with the transition.

Change is a period of uncertainty and a challenge to your ability to plan ahead and predict what the future holds for you. However, if you are able to identify the connections between your

Worksheet 1: Thoughts and Feelings about Change

Think about an organizational change that affected you. In the table below, record the thoughts and feelings that accompanied this change.

Change	Thoughts about the Change	Feelings Generated by Thoughts

This exercise is not meant to prove that there is no need to worry during an organizational change. Instead, it is meant to create a connection between the organizational change and the powerful thoughts and feelings that this change creates. Identifying the connection between a change and the impact that change has on you is the first step in managing the transition.

This worksheet will help you identify the thoughts and feelings that the change within your organization had on you. You can use this worksheet whenever you are anticipating or involved in a corporate change, as it will help you recognize the impact of the change by identifying your emotional reaction to it. Once you have identified the thoughts and feelings that the change has brought about, you are closer to being able to successfully manage the transition.

Did the thoughts that you recorded show that you began to doubt your skills as a result of the change? Did your feelings indicate that you felt you were losing more than you could possibly gain from the change? Is there a pattern of uncertainty throughout these thoughts and feelings?

thoughts and feelings and the impact the change has upon you, you will be more willing to move ahead into the new beginning.

The Ending Stage

The first stage of transition that you must manage is the ending. With every transition, there is an ending to the way things

used to be. To successfully adapt to organizational change in this stage, you must acknowledge what is ending, recognize the change, and describe the thoughts and feelings associated with that ending. This is especially necessary when the change is difficult or when you are ambivalent about the change. The ending is the transitional stage that many leaders skip, either consciously because they attempt to quickly move ahead without taking note of what has changed, or unconsciously because they think the change itself is the ending. However, making a new beginning is not the same as acknowledging and experiencing the ending stage. In fact, it is quite the opposite. To make a new beginning, you must adapt to change by recognizing the end of the old way.

Suppose that you have worked for years as an executive in a large and complex nonprofit organization. The area you lead is being spun off as its own entity and purchased by a for-profit corporation. You play a role in that change, gaining even greater leadership responsibilities, but for a changed entity with entirely new business and operational models. To adapt to that change, you have to make a transition. Start by recognizing the ending that has occurred and experiencing the thoughts and feelings associated with it. What do you feel, and what are the thoughts associated with these feelings? Do you feel anger or sadness? Are you anxious or depressed?

If you actually were the leader in the preceding example, you might have experienced feelings and thoughts such as those shown in Figure 2, Thoughts and Feelings about Endings, even if you had played a role in the change.

Figure 2: Thoughts and Feelings about Endings

Thoughts	Feelings
I was dedicated to working in the nonprofit sector, but now I'm forced to work in a for-profit corporation. I feel betrayed.	anger
I had always hoped to retire as the CEO of a nonprofit, but now…	sadness
I am still doing nonprofit work; this change is just a technicality.	denial
If I can just accept the mission, I don't really care about profit.	bargaining
Everyone will think I am going against my values. How can I hold my head high?	anxiety
I am not true to myself anymore; I'm living a lie.	depression
This new business is going to create entirely new opportunities for me.	anticipation
I am finally going to be paid what I deserve.	excitement

Change is a period of uncertainty and a challenge to your ability to plan ahead and predict what the future holds for you.

Change raises questions that have no obvious answers and problems with no easy solutions. Further, when change occurs, it is tempting to fear the worst and adopt a sense of dread, mainly because the methods, customs, and models with which you were familiar and in which you had expertise are no longer the standards. If these feelings are left unresolved, they can lead managers who are otherwise successful to derail.

By moving through the ending stage and focusing on the thoughts and feelings that this stage of the transition generates in you, you can move from reacting to change toward managing a transition. Marking the ending is perhaps the biggest leap forward in the process of managing the transition because it helps you do the following:

- factually identify who is losing what
- emotionally identify who is losing what
- accept the reality of the change
- acknowledge the emotions of the change
- grieve
- treat the past with respect
- carry the past forward into the future

None of these accomplishments are possible, however, if you do not mark the ending of the way things used to be. When you fail to acknowledge the ending and you fail to actively manage and openly acknowledge the emotional impacts that the change has had on you, you allow the change to drive your thoughts, feelings,

In order to progress through the ending stage to the next stage of transition, you must fully experience the change as an ending. The following strategies can help you move through the ending stage and to the second stage of transition, the neutral zone:

- **Listen.** Learn all you can about the nature of the change without first judging it.
- **Make an inventory.** Take stock of who is losing what.
- **Define.** Color in the precise details of what is over and what is not.
- **Acknowledge.** Admit to yourself and others that the change has occurred.
- **Inquire.** Actively seek information from all relevant sources about the change.
- **Share.** Let others know the facts and feelings that you have about the change.
- **Signify.** Mark the ending in a meaningful way.
- **Identify.** Take note of what has been lost and what has been gained.

and actions. By marking the ending, however, you begin the process of taking control and managing the transition.

Although the three stages of transition are distinct, you can experience all of them at the same time. In fact, during a period of transition, the stages will ebb and flow, and your thoughts and feelings may move among them, but you must fully experience the ending stage and be emotionally prepared to enter the next stage. Worksheet 2, Thoughts and Feelings about Endings, will help you do this. This preparedness will increase the likelihood that you can manage your transition successfully and adapt to organizational change.

Worksheet 2: Thoughts and Feelings about Endings

Consider the last significant job change you experienced (this could be a position change, a team change, or a new project that forced you to rethink your current strategies).

What was the change?
How did you first think and feel about the change?
How did you deal with the ending of the old way?
Did you use any of the ending strategies? If not, how did you attempt to manage the transition?
What was the result of your efforts to manage the transition?
After reviewing your findings, is there anything you would do differently if facing that same change again?

The Neutral Zone

The second stage of transition that you must recognize and experience is the neutral zone—the space between the old reality and the new. It's the time when the old way is gone, but the new way is still unfamiliar and perhaps even uncomfortable. To successfully adapt to organizational change in the neutral zone, recognize the uncertainty associated with change and experience the thoughts and feelings associated with that uncertainty.

Consider this example of a change: You work as an executive in a manufacturing concern that produces products in five US plants. The company has decided to close all but one plant and consolidate production in an overseas facility. You retain your leadership role, but in a changed entity with new customs, relationships, and bureaucracies that are completely unfamiliar to you. To adapt to change and continue your transition, recognize the neutral zone you are in and experience the thoughts and feelings associated with it. What do you feel, and what thoughts are associated with these feelings? Do you feel doubtful or uncertain? Are you confused or unproductive?

If you were the executive in this example, you may have experienced feelings and thoughts such as those indicated in Figure 3, Thoughts and Feelings about the Neutral Zone.

Figure 3: Thoughts and Feelings about the Neutral Zone

Thoughts	Feelings
I don't know where to go or whom to talk to anymore!	untethered
All my old tricks are no longer sure things. I don't know whether they will work in this new environment.	doubtful
At least I knew how to work with my labor union representatives. Now I'm not sure what I'm doing.	uncertain
I can't tell from their reactions whether my overseas staff members agree or disagree with me. I can't read them at all.	confused
Everything is so new to me; I feel as if it's one step forward and two steps back.	unproductive
All my old weaknesses are reemerging. I feel as if I'm back to square one.	unskilled

Moving through the neutral zone is possibly the most uncomfortable transition stage, but focusing on the thoughts and feelings of this stage can assist you in the move from reacting to change toward successfully managing the transition. To accomplish this move, adopt the following strategies:

- **Accept.** Realize that uncertainty is an integral stage between an ending and a new beginning. Don't expect to know everything or to be perfect.

- **Plan.** Set short-term goals to move through uncertainty and advance toward a new beginning. Take stock of what you need to accomplish those goals and identify opportunities that will help you move forward.

- **Balance.** Keep your feet. Look backward to the ending and acknowledge what you had. Look forward to the beginning and the possibilities it could create.

- **Anchor.** Connect to your values. When you feel uncertain and confused, feelings characteristic of the neutral zone, your personal values can remind you of how you got where you are and can provide direction.

Although accepting, planning, and balancing are all effective strategies, the anchoring strategy can be particularly useful in helping you navigate the neutral zone. When negotiating the neutral zone using the anchoring strategy, take stock of your personal values so that you can better understand what you have lost and what you might gain. This will allow you to envision the benefits that change might bring, put aside the negative or uncertain feelings that are an integral part of this stage, and make way for a more positive outlook in the new beginning stage. When taking stock of your personal values, keep in mind that these values are your anchor because they remain with you despite the changes happening around you. These core beliefs that you hold true are reflected in your behavior; they are about what is important in your life and are deep-seated and pervasive standards that influence nearly every aspect of your actions.

By taking stock of your personal values, you can project the values that are most important for you and the benefits that would be most beneficial for you to gain from the corporate change. Although many people espouse values as important, they sometimes behave in ways that don't support those beliefs. For example, if you select health as an important value but do not eat right and exercise, then health is probably not that

---

By taking stock of your personal values, you can project the values that are most important for you and the benefits that would be most beneficial for you to gain.

---

important to you. If you value cooperation at work but during tense organizational change blame your team when tasks are not met instead of working with team members to lead them toward the goal, then cooperation is not a value you are practicing. If you want to find your personal values that will anchor you in the neutral zone, you must first be honest with yourself.

It is also important that you take stock of your organization's values. These organizational values are an integral component of organizational culture, and just as on an individual basis, there are espoused values, which often appear in mission statements and value statements, and there are actual behaviorally supported values. Some are congruent, and some may be in contrast. For example, the organization may say it values an open-door policy, yet many doors are closed or are guarded by assistants. Therefore, just as with your personal values, you want to be honest about what organizational values are actually being practiced. Doing so will allow you to better understand what the organization lost in the ending and what it might gain in the new beginning. Additionally, by compiling the organization's values, you can align your values with the organization's to better see how you figure into the new corporate culture.

Worksheet 3, Thoughts and Feelings about the Neutral Zone, will help you deal with personal and organizational values.

The neutral zone is a time of uncertainty but also an opportunity to align yourself with your new organization and to recognize the potential that you have within the new organizational structure. The neutral zone will help you prepare for and determine what benefits you think you will gain from the new beginning.

Your success as a leader will very likely depend on how well you deal with change.

Worksheet 3: Thoughts and Feelings about the Neutral Zone

In the table below, list the values that are important to you personally and then list the values that are important to your organization.

Values Important to You	Values Important to Your Organization

Compare the lists and make notes about any concerns you may have. Do you see gaps between your values and the values you believe are reflected in the organization? If so, it may be appropriate for you to attempt to enact these values if they are appropriate for your organization.

Now that you understand your values and those of your organization and you have values that you believe should be enacted as a part of the organizational culture, you can begin to plan your approach to this and the next organizational change that you may be faced with.

Organizational Values

The following are some of the most prevalent values demonstrated by top organizations:

health—being physically and mentally well

wealth—making money, getting rich

family happiness—having a satisfying relationship with those you live with

friendship—close relationships with others

involvement—participating with others, belonging

loyalty—duty, respectfulness, obedience

responsibility—accountability for results

helpfulness—assisting others, improving society

self-respect—pride, sense of personal identity

cooperation—working well with others, teamwork

economic security—steady and adequate income, stable employment

spirit—strong religious or spiritual beliefs

order—tranquility, stability

achievement—sense of accomplishment, mastery

inner harmony—being at peace with yourself

balance—lifestyle that incorporates time for self, family, community, and work

pleasure—fun, laughs, leisurely lifestyle

recognition—respect from others, status

affection—caring, close personal relationships

creativity—being imaginative, being innovative

advancement—promotion

wisdom—understanding life, discovering knowledge

personal development—use of potential

adventure—new and challenging experiences, risk taking

integrity—standing up for beliefs

fame—being well-known

freedom—independence, autonomy

competitiveness—winning, being right

The New Beginning Stage

Once you have experienced an ending and navigated through the neutral zone, the next stage is the new beginning. It's the start of

something new and the time when the old way is gone and you have come to terms with what benefits you and the organization can expect from the change. But the new way is just beginning. To successfully adapt to organizational change in the new beginning, recognize the thoughts and feelings associated with it.

Consider this example of a change in market. You work as an executive in a consumer products company with a dominating market share. You maintain that edge by extending existing practices and making slight adjustments that leverage current strengths. A new, well-funded competitor launches an aggressive campaign to gain market share. You retain your leadership role, but in a changed entity that must move from thoughtful reaction to forceful action.

If you were the executive in this example, you may have experienced feelings and thoughts such as those shown in Figure 4, Thoughts and Feelings about the New Beginning.

Figure 4: Thoughts and Feelings about the New Beginning

Thoughts	Feelings
I feel as I did when I was first promoted to senior management.	recognition
I don't know if I can do this.	hesitation
It's now or never. Uh-oh, here we go.	reluctance

As you are faced with the new beginning, you will be able to validate the values that you identified for yourself and your organization in the neutral zone. This validation will help ensure that both you and the organization reap rewards from the change.

When moving through the new beginning, take stock of what the new post-change organization actually looks like and experience the fresh start it represents. To do so, adopt the following strategies:

- **Envision.** Paint a picture of the new beginning. Imagine what it looks and feels like. Symbolize the new beginning in words, images, and thoughts.
- **Share.** Give everyone a part in the new beginning; find a place for all relevant parties to the change.
- **Plan.** Create strategies for tackling new problems and meeting new challenges.
- **Confirm.** Reemphasize the reason for the change and recognize that reason as why you are beginning anew.
- **Celebrate.** Find ways to mark your successes.

The new beginning is an opportunity. You have developed goals and ideals for the new organization, and you have a strong vision of what lies ahead. As part of realizing the opportunity that a new beginning brings, you must do the following:

- Recognize that change is a dynamic process. You and the organization will continue to experience change. You will continue to make transitions. Today's mismatch may be tomorrow's match.

- Find common ground. Maximize the match between your values and the values of the organization by linking your daily activities to those common standards. Seek out work in the organization that echoes your values.

- Find other sources to support your values. If work does not meet your need for honoring specific values of personal importance, then look for that support in your personal relationships and your nonwork activities.

Although the new beginning is a time of change, it is also an opportunity for creating strategies for tackling new problems and meeting new challenges. This is the stage where you take stock of what the new organization actually looks like and determine your role within it.

The Process of Transition

Transitions are movements from the ending, through the neutral zone, and into a new beginning. Although each stage of a transition occurs during a distinct time period, each phase somewhat overlaps the others. Individuals experience organizational change in a myriad of ways. These experiences depend upon the person's placement within the organization and the give-and-take between what the person feels has been lost and gained, as well as the type of organizational changes and shifts that occur.

The following example illustrates how you might experience an organizational change through each stage of transition. You work as an executive in a long-established telecommunications company with a large number of seasoned employees and a deep well of traditional business practices. Business suits, closed office doors, and formal meetings with detailed agendas mark the environment. A fast-growing company, populated by mostly young employees with a bias toward innovation and action, buys out the company. Jeans, T-shirts, open work areas, and hallway meetings mark the new environment. You retain a leadership role in a changed entity with a different way of looking at, evaluating, and doing things.

Figure 5, Strategies for Each Stage, illustrates the stages of transition, the thoughts that are prevalent in each stage, the feelings that these thoughts generate, and the strategies for managing each.

A Look to Culture

One way to clarify your perception of the organization is to describe it using metaphors, adjectives, and verbs. CCL's Leadership Metaphor Explorer, through the use of descriptive metaphors to represent leadership styles, enables creative, insightful conversations in groups of people about three topics. It covers the kinds of leadership those groups presently have or practice, the kinds of leadership they need in the future, and how to develop those required forms of leadership—both personally as one's leadership style and collectively as a shared leadership culture. While this may seem unusual on the surface, the responses

Figure 5: Strategies for Each Stage

Stages	Thoughts	Feelings	Strategies
Ending	I've been left behind; I'm a dinosaur.	fear of being obsolete	Mark the ending by identifying what is over and what was lost but also what is not over and what is not lost. Listen and gather information.
Neutral zone	I can't be as loose and creative as these new guys. I feel as if I'm starting all over again.	frustration	Don't expect perfection. Set reasonable short-term goals and tackle them.
New beginning	These guys need an old-style number cruncher like me.	reluctance, acceptance	Understand why the company had to change; jump into the new flow with a plan to enjoy and participate with everyone involved.

say a lot about how individuals perceive their organizational culture. Moreover, understanding how others perceive the new organizational culture will assist you in aligning your transitional strategies so that they are beneficial to you and to your organization.

Organizational change can be difficult. In order to manage transition, you must deal with your own personal uncertainty and resistance to change, which CCL research has shown is a factor in executive success. Beyond this, however, you will have

Worksheet 4: Which Metaphor Best Fits Your Organization?

Take a moment to consider your organizational changes in terms of the following metaphors. These cards are taken from Leadership Metaphor Explorer, a dynamic tool developed by CCL in order to stimulate and inspire discussions on leadership in organizations:

Ambitious Pioneers

Cave Dwellers

Circle of Inclusion

Community of Strangers

Fierce Dinosaurs

Geese Flying in Formation

1. What metaphor or combination of metaphors best describes your organization's culture?

2. What five adjectives (not necessarily from the above cards) best describe your organization?

3. What five verbs best fit your organization? What behaviors do you observe among others in the organization that support your answers?

4. How do you feel about the answers you have given?

After you have answered these questions, ask others within your organization these same questions and determine whether they share your perceptions. Then reexamine the organizational values you listed in Worksheet 3 in comparison to the way that others have described the organization. What new possibilities does this create?

to help other people deal with their thoughts and feelings, and the approaches that you have learned in this guidebook—looking at thoughts and feelings in each of the stages of transition—will help you face this challenge.

Background

William Bridges has been a leader in the field of transition management since his book *Transitions: Making Sense of Life's Changes* was first published in 1980 (second edition, 2004). For many years, he has worked with organizations to help them get their employees through the transitions they have to make with less distress and disruption. That work was the basis of his 1991 book *Managing Transitions: Making the Most of Change* (third edition, 2009). With the publication of *JobShift: How to Prosper in a Workplace Without Jobs* in 1994 and *Creating You & Co.: Learn to Think Like the CEO of Your Own Career* in 1997, he has become one of the most widely read and quoted experts on what is happening to jobs in today's organizations and on new strategies that individuals must find to work.

The Center for Creative Leadership has conducted extensive research on derailment, contrasting those people who make it to the top with those who derail. These studies have identified characteristics that mark the difference between managers who continue to be considered highly promotable and those who leave an organization involuntarily or reach a plateau. This research has been subsequently confirmed by data from Benchmarks, CCL's comprehensive 360-degree assessment tool that identifies strengths and development needs, encourages and guides change, and offers strategic insights for middle to upper-level managers and executives.

Suggested Resources

Bridges, W. (2009). *Managing transitions: Making the most of change* (3rd ed.). Boston, MA: Da Capo Press.

Bunker, K. A. (2008). *Responses to change: Helping people manage transition.* Greensboro, NC: Center for Creative Leadership.

Bunker, K. A., & Wakefield, M. (2005). *Leading with authenticity in times of transition.* Greensboro, NC: Center for Creative Leadership.

Bunker, K. A., & Wakefield, M. (2010). Leading through transitions [Facilitator's guide set]. San Francisco, CA: Pfeiffer.

Calarco, A., & Gurvis, J. (2006). *Adaptability: Responding effectively to change.* Greensboro, NC: Center for Creative Leadership.

Leslie, J. B., & Van Velsor, E. (1996). *A look at derailment today: North America and Europe.* Greensboro, NC: Center for Creative Leadership.

Lombardo, M. M., & Eichinger, R. W. (1989). *Preventing derailment: What to do before it's too late.* Greensboro, NC: Center for Creative Leadership.

Palus, C. J., & Horth, D. M. (2012). Leadership metaphor explorer: Creative conversations for better leadership [Card deck and facilitator's guide]. Greensboro, NC: Center for Creative Leadership.

Rush, S. (Ed.). (2012). *On leading in times of change.* Greensboro, NC: Center for Creative Leadership.

Ordering Information

TO GET MORE INFORMATION, TO ORDER OTHER IDEAS INTO ACTION GUIDEBOOKS, OR TO FIND OUT ABOUT BULK-ORDER DISCOUNTS, PLEASE CONTACT US BY PHONE AT 336-545-2810 OR VISIT OUR ONLINE BOOKSTORE AT WWW.CCL.ORG/GUIDEBOOKS.